SECRETS

WHEN YOU RUN YOUR FINGERS THROUGH THEIR HAIR

By Stacie Harmon
Written with Jennifer Christiansen
Illustrations by Doug MacGregor

ISBN: 1470077345
ISBN-13: 978-1470077341

Dedicated to my mother, DeDe, who has, by far, been my biggest source of support. She is my mentor as she, herself, stood day after day behind the chair to provide for my brother and me. She taught me how to make my job fun.

"My Momma always told me... men are like linoleum floors, lay them just right and you can walk all over them for the next thirty years."

Grace Kelly: Grace Under Fire 1993

ACKNOWLEDGMENTS

My deepest appreciation to Jennifer Christiansen. When I sat down with Jen and shared my idea, she did what any great girlfriend would do, encouraged and offered to assist. She has given this book the flair that makes me want to pick it up and read it again and again. This collaboration has certainly been a labor of love for both of us.

To Danette De Rouin, for working hours upon hours to perfect this book cover. Your efforts are more than appreciated, you are a star.

To Laurel Robinson, for your fine editing along the way and your never ending patience especially towards the end when I sent one page at a time.

To Doug MacGregor, whose time and artistic talents are invaluable. His illustrations have given this book humor, bringing it to life like no one else…

Heartfelt gratitude:

To both sets of parents for providing the unconditional love and support I constantly needed to pull off this goal.

To my daughter, Savannah, who has shown such enthusiasm on a subject that most children her age would not understand. She is a true wise one and without her I would still be wandering the world without purpose. I love you my precious baby girl.

To her daddy, Scott, for tolerating so much and for giving me the opportunity to love deeply and write about the experience… Thank you most of all, Scott, for the most precious gift in the world - our daughter.

To my younger brother, Rick, who has always thought his big sister could accomplish anything. Consequently, giving me self confidence and wings to truly fly.

To Maxwell, for his sense of adventure and for passionately pushing me to finish this feat. Thank you, MT, for gently encouraging me everyday with your unwavering love and affection.

To all my fellow stylists that share my passion for the craft and for standing behind their clients for long hours at a time listening … just listening.

And most of all… To my clients, who over the years have shared their lives in such an intimate setting. They say behind every great man stands a greater woman? But, not in this case, it's because I stood behind you, that I am a greater woman. Thank you, thank you.

INTRODUCTION

From the Air to the Chair

Soaring from Los Angeles to New York on the wings of prestigious MGM Grand Air's Boeing 727 was quite the ride. I was a flight attendant for the luxury airline, and the nineties practically flew by in a blur of celebrities, champagne, caviar, and constant attention. At a ratio of five flight attendants to thirty-five passengers, each trip was an intimate adventure. Experiencing a lifestyle that mirrored that of a supermodel, I rubbed elbows with famous athletes, world-renowned music stars, and CEOs of Fortune 500 companies. I still marvel at the lavish invitations we collected from our passengers. In nine short years, I went through three passports, each loaded with stamps from locations all over Europe, Russia, Asia, the Middle East, and the Mediterranean.

So why would anyone give up traveling around the world with celebrities such as Rod Stewart, Michael Jackson, Phil Collins, U2, Guns N' Roses, and the Rolling Stones to stand in one place, especially when that place was behind a man?

The truth is that I wanted more. The stability of a home, friends, and a family of my own didn't seem possible with that jet-set lifestyle. My romantic life, although wonderfully thrilling, was beginning to leave me feeling vaguely unfulfilled. Instead of whining about Mr. So-Close-But-No-Cigar, I was determined to take a more positive approach. I wanted to educate myself on what made men tick, and the best way to do that was to be up close and personal with them. And as luck would have it, I knew exactly where to begin.When I was fourteen years old, my mother opened a men's salon in Thousand Oaks, California. My first job was sweeping hair clippings, folding towels, and occasionally taking appointments for the stylists. After a few years of success, my mother decided to expand the business to cater to women as well. The new manicuring stations, facial rooms, and tanning beds attracted female customers in droves, but I mourned for the days when the stimulating banter of men filled the air.

When my mother retired, I downsized and brought the salon back to its former all-male glory. Richard Michael's Salon, named after my younger brother who was a high-fashion international model known for his hair, was a place that men loved to go. Conveniently nestled between companies such as J. D. Power & Associates, Net Zero, and Pratt & Whitney Rocketdyne, the salon never lacked clientele. The stylists were not only talented, but also friendly and easy on the eyes. We provided cold beer and Esquire instead of diet soda and Cosmopolitan.

Creating a hair salon exclusively for men was an ideal niche business. Low overhead, no gossip, no acrylic nail odor, easy money, and an endless stream of compliments is what I imagined, but I got something even more precious: a wealth of information. Like your neighborhood bartender, the men told me everything.

And once I began listening … really listening … I reached the conclusion that … *sometimes … it's not just* ***his*** *fault!*

SECRETS MEN SHARE

...When you Run Your Fingers Through Their Hair

CHAPTER 1
Getting to the Roots

The fairest thing in nature, a flower,
still has its roots in earth and manure.
—D. H. Lawrence

"Can you squeeze Walter in today?"

Heather, my receptionist, assistant, and savior, met me at the door with my appointment book. Although she was petite, she had no trouble keeping up with my long stride. I was already ten minutes late, but she easily followed my mad dash.

"I can do it after Peter," I said after a quick glance at the book. "He only has half a head."

Meaning, he has hair only around the outer banks. The cul-de-sac cut.

The salon was already pumping with five other stylists and their clients. I took a deep breath, inhaling the heavenly scent of men's cologne. My day was jam-packed with seventeen heads, four of which were getting color.

Receiving constant attention was the main reason I had chosen this job, but my first client of the day was almost more than I could handle.

George

"I'll be right with you, George!" I said. He was waiting in the foyer, reading the front page of the *Wall Street Journal.*_

After putting my things at my station, I went into the back room. I wrapped myself in the standard apron and washed my hands. Before going back out, I took another deep breath. *I'm ready for ya!*

"You look nice, Stacie," he said as I laid him back in the shampoo chair.

"Thanks! I just got these shoes, and of course I had to find something to wear with them. That's why I was late this morning. Sorry if I kept you too long."

"You can make up for it with an extra scalp massage," he said. After the first wash, he actually had the nerve to ask to be shampooed again. "Either you didn't scrub hard enough or you're wearing a tighter bra. The entertainment is weak this time."

I rolled my eyes and prayed for the strength to refrain from spraying the water straight up his nose.

George wasn't the only client to make comments like these. What was it with men?

Bus Stop

One day at a bus stop, there was a girl who was wearing a skintight miniskirt. When the bus arrived and it was her turn to get on, she realized that her skirt was so tight she couldn't get her foot high enough to reach the step.

Thinking it would give her enough slack to raise her leg, she reached back and unzipped her skirt a little. She still could not reach the step. Embarrassed, she reached back once again to unzip it a little more. Still, she couldn't reach the step.

So, with her skirt zipper halfway down, she reached back and unzipped her skirt all the way. Thinking that she could get on the step now, she lifted up her leg only to realize that she still couldn't reach the step.

So, seeing how embarrassed the girl was, the man standing behind her put his hands around her waist and lifted her up on to the first step of the bus. The girl turned around furiously and said, "How dare you touch my body that way, I don't even know you!"

Shocked, the man said, "Well, ma'am, after you reached around and unzipped my fly three times, I kinda figured that we were friends."

Steve

"Steve, I haven't seen you in a while. What have you been up to?" I asked my second appointment of the day.

Seeming to ignore the question, he plopped down in my chair with an apologetic look on his face. Then he proceeded to tell me about his indiscretions.

Steve must have been forty-five years old and happily married with two kids and a dog, but as I said, I was like the neighborhood bartender in that my clients felt they could tell me anything. He rambled on about how sorry he was, saying that he didn't intend to pursue the relationship any further.

"How did your wife take it?" I asked.

"She doesn't know. Please don't say a word," he pleaded.

I must have heard this a gazillion times in my career, but this story ended a little differently. Once I discovered

I was the one he had cheated on, it began to make sense why he was so apologetic.

"My buddy gave me the phone number of some Hollywood hairstylist who supposedly worked while wearing some super-hot clothes. So one day, when I looked in my rearview mirror at the hair covering my ears, I thought it was now or never."

"Mmm … hmm …," I said absently.

"So I rang the number and a soft, sexy voice answered," he said. "I could barely get the words out without stuttering, but I managed to tell her that a friend had referred me. When she asked what exactly my friend had told me, I just about lost it." He grinned sheepishly. "I told her that I'd heard she gave good head."

That got my attention. "You what? I better put my scissors down for a minute."

"I didn't mean it," he said. "I guess it was kind of a Freudian slip. Anyway, I corrected myself and said 'good haircuts,' but the odd thing was that she wasn't upset. She actually laughed and told me my friend was right. At that point I didn't even know which one she was talking about, head or hair."

"Okay," I said as I picked up where I had left off on the trim. "So of course you ended up going, right?"

"Uh huh. Right away, actually. When she opened the door, all I saw were a pair of dark, mysterious eyes and this unbelievably sexy chocolate-brown hair. Almost black, actually. At that point, all I could think was *Thank God I had the forethought to spray some Binaca in my mouth.*" He forced a laugh.

I laughed along with him. "So what happened? Did she mess up the cut or something?" There had to be some reason why he had come crawling back to me.

"Well … uh … no … The cut was fine. It's what she did next," he said. "She didn't say anything. Just draped the cape around me and handed me a mirror. I was clueless. I mean, she hadn't even done anything yet. I just sat there at first until she motioned to her skirt and tilted the mirror down, and that's when I discovered she had no panties on! That was a detail my friend had left out!"

He finished the story by describing how he had sat there in uncomfortable silence the entire time, stunned and embarrassed. "As much of a wow factor as it was, the idea was more intriguing than the actual experience," he said, admiring himself in the mirror. "I am never going back there. Anyway, your talent and conversation are much more stimulating."

He was so lucky that I didn't snip off his ear.

Jack

Trapped under my cape as if locked in a Catholic confessional booth, Jack just started spilling.

"Did you know they can check the DNA of a baby while it's still in the womb?" he asked.

Jack was fifty-one years old, married to his high school sweetheart, and had four children. He was a managing member of an elite law firm and took at least three vacations a year: one with his wife, one with his family, and one with the boys, either golfing or fishing.

I envied his wife. She always dressed to the nines, drove nice cars, and got her hair and nails done once a week.

Yet here it came …

"How do you know that, Jack?" I asked. "Better yet, *why* do you know this? Is one of your daughters pregnant?"

"Not one of my daughters, dear. One of my girlfriends."

"What!" I screeched, keeping a tight hold on my scissors. "Are you kidding me? Are you insane? Have you lost your mind? You have the life of Riley, and you're telling me you've been cheating on your wife?"

"Shh … unfaithful, Stacie, unfaithful!" he said, looking around to see if anyone could overhear our conversation.

"Is there a difference?"

"Thirty years married to the same woman is a long time, Stacie, but you wouldn't know that yet."

"How would you feel if she had a boyfriend?" I asked.

"She probably does. We just don't talk about it," he said. "I don't really want to know. We wouldn't want to upset the wagon, if you know what I mean. Our kids depend on us. We went through counseling, and the therapist gave us some great advice. He said that when the honeymoon is over, marriage becomes a corporation. It's the Williams Corporation. You begin to make decisions with this in mind. What's best for the corporation is the question. In my case, not discussing infidelity is what is best for our corporation."

"Wow. What an eye-opener," I said, suddenly feeling very naive.

"Don't get me wrong," he said. "Not every marriage is like this. It just works for us. So about the baby ..."

Fact

"Approximately 40 percent of men seek sexual satisfaction outside their relationships," estimates Kat Hertlein, PhD, marriage and family therapist and professor of human development at the University of Nevada, Las Vegas.

The number hasn't changed much since the 1950s, when the famous Kinsey sex study found that 50 percent of U.S. men cheat at some point in their marriages. What my clients have shared over the years validates and supports Kinsey's theory of:

Why They Cheat

1. **Boredom: It's the thrill.** Often married men who cheat can't quite explain their motivation. They just find themselves compelled to bust out of their day-to-day routine in search of something new.

2. **Escape: His wife is a nag.** Perhaps nothing will drive a married man into the arms of another woman faster than a pestering wife.

3. **Attraction: He has lost the loving feeling.** If his wife has gained weight or stopped taking care of herself, a man will begin looking at other women.

4. **Opportunity: He's more powerful than when he got married.** Women are attracted to men who have power and status, so those men have plenty of opportunities. New success brings new temptation. Power wives, beware! Many of my clients concur. If you are married to a high-profile guy, the possibility that he will wander is increased.

5. **Economics: It's cheaper than a divorce.** He's unhappy with his mate, but getting a divorce is expensive.

6. **Love: He was never in love with her in the first place.** He may have married because of pressure from family, early pregnancy, or to keep up with his friends.

Whatever the excuse is for doing the extramarital mambo, it is just that—an excuse. An excuse that comes with deep roots. If you can get to those roots, you may have a chance of changing his behavior and landing in the other percentile.

The best advice is to really study your man before you commit your heart.

"Men have two emotions: Hungry and Horny. If you see him without an erection, make him a sandwich."

-Unknown

"Holding on to youth can
be a hair-raising adventure!"

CHAPTER 2
The Bald Truth

Truth is like the sun. You can shut it out
for a time, but it ain't goin' away.
—Elvis Presley

One of my favorite clients was Hale, a strapping gentleman with sandy brown hair and a manicured mustache who came in every month like clockwork. I secretly referred to him as "Goose" as in my *Top Gun* wingman.

Ironically, Goose was a contract pilot who sold custom yachts at a nearby brokerage on days he was not flying. In his late fifties, he still stood tall at over six feet five inches. Like most successful men, Goose was particular about his hair and very much stuck in his ways. Men of that type often find something that works and continue rolling with it without change.

A stylist in the past suggested he grow his hair a little longer on one side so he could sweep it over the top to camouflage his balding hairline. When he approached the shop one Friday, I thought we were going to lose him to the cloudy, gray skies. As he reached for the handle of the door, a huge gust of wind caught him from the side causing the wing to stand up at attention. I tried not to laugh as I watched his head jerk over to the side.

Over the years, I had many clients who insisted on this style. I reluctantly did it for them, but never put much thought into how the hair sprayed comb-over would perform in the wind. Until Goose. Every time I saw him after that, the image of Chevy Chase in the movie *Fletch* flashed in my mind. "He's 6'5". 6'9" with the afro." Goose's disastrous-'do also caused me to worry about my insurance premium, due to the newfound flight risk from the comb-over.

When I told him what I had witnessed, he was embarrassed. My candidness, however, caused him to agree to cut it off. He had a hard time getting used to it, but finally admitted he was complimented so much that he wondered what people had thought before. I was able to call my insurance company to tell them my client was no longer a flight risk.

Fret not your hair turning gray, it could turn loose!

Leonard

Even though Leonard was a respectable architect and longtime client, he always acted as if I was not paying close enough attention to his stories. He had to be looking at me whenever he talked, which is uncomfortable at the shampoo bowl because of the proximity of faces. Most clients relaxed their eyelids and focused elsewhere, the same way I would while in the dentist's chair, but not Leonard. Not even the occasional splash of soap in his eye could deter him. Even worse was the fact that he was also a toucher. Usually I smiled politely when he reached up and touched my hip to make sure I was still listening, but one time his hand landed squarely on my bum as I turned to grab some conditioner.

Whoa. I knew that since I hadn't made it to the gym that day or had ample opportunity to clench and tighten, it must have felt soft. We all know that some flex time is needed to get the High & Tight Ass we all think we have. When I looked down and saw him wink, however, I realized that the "accident" had been more intentional than I had originally thought. Disgusted, I decided to set an all-time speed record for the rest of his appointment, but that didn't stop him from trying more accidental gestures again at my chair.

"Look in the mirror, Leonard," I demanded as I thought of all the damage my shears could do to his little pug nose.

The truth is that men will do as much as they can get away with, so I recommend short leashes and solid boundaries. The next time Leonard came in, I told him that touching would cost him extra. From the way he tipped, I knew that would work.

Piggy Bank

As a painless way to save money, a young couple arranged that every time they have sex the husband puts his pocket change into a china piggy bank on the bedside table. One night while being unusually athletic, he accidentally knocked the bank to the floor where it smashes. To his surprise, among the masses of coins, there are handfuls of five and ten dollar bills. He asks his wife what's up. "Well," she replied, "Not everyone is as cheap as you are."

Vaughn

"I guess I was getting a wee bit demanding with me wife," Vaughn said. "After one particularly rough day at work, I rather impolitely asked her to rub me feet."

"Ooh … that's not good," I said. With his English accent and cynical sense of humor, Vaughn's stories usually had me cracking up before my shears touched a hair on his head, and obviously this time was not going to be an exception.

"When she returned from the loo with the peppermint foot rub and began to rub me shins with a smile, I thought to meself, *Brilliant—the full treatment tonight.* After a few sniffs, though, I realized it wasn't the minty scent I remembered."

"I don't even think I want to know, Vaughn," I said, already imagining the many possibilities.

"Before I could even ask about the change, she laid a chilled washcloth over the top of me legs. With one silly swipe the thing was covered with dark brown leg hair."

"Oh my gosh!" As hard as I tried, I couldn't prevent the bubbles of laughter from escaping my lips.

"It's all right. You can laugh, Stacie," he said after seeing the apologetic smile spreading across my face. "That's what the wife did as she walked out of the room with a cloth that looked like she'd skinned a bloody beaver. After that I learned to show a little more compassion when asking her for something. The tops of me legs were as bare as a baby's bum, and I didn't have the guts to ask her to do the rest to match. Needless to say, trousers replaced my usual shorts for a bit."

Now, that was a wife who knew how to manage her man.

Frank

Frank, a bicyclist in his free time, wore spandex sport shorts to his appointments, even when no bike was in sight.

"Frank, did you ride your bike here?" I asked each time he visited. "I see you have your bike shorts on."

The answer was always the same: a hug. A tight hug during which he never failed to take advantage of the opportunity to press his hips forward. Even though I have always been a naturally affectionate person, his extra hip thrust that day grossed me out. I certainly didn't need to feel that—not Frank's, anyway. From that day on, he barely got a pat on the back.

Other clients learned early on how to score an extra hug from me. They brought gestures of appreciation such as chocolate, wine, or the almighty vanilla latte. For those things, they deserved more than a hug, but I always kept it professional.

Like the proverbial dog, men love attention. If you can get their tail to wag with praise, they're yours. So, women, bark less to get your man to wag more.

Since I was consistently ten minutes behind on my appointments, my clients passed the time in different ways. Some came in ten minutes late, and others paced outside while making phone calls. They dealt with it because they knew they would be treated like kings once they were in my chair. I made sure every client felt as handsome and desirable as any Hollywood leading man.

If more women gave their man this kind of attention, there would be less infidelity and a lot more tail wagging. It doesn't take much to give him a compliment. Touch him in an unexpected area, such as behind the ears (again like a dog). Rub his shoulders, but only for a few minutes to leave him wanting more. A woman's touch is intoxicating. If you don't give him attention, someone else will. Then before you know it, he will be following *her* around.

Joe

From the front door I saw Joe sitting in a puddle of cold sweat. His hands were clutching the armrests of his salon chair, turning his knuckles stark white.

"Wha … what ... what is going on?" I said as I reached the station.

Suzanne threw her chin over her right shoulder. "Come check it out," she said with a smile. "This morning I picked up this new waxing kit for half off. Now we can wax the hair off the back of their necks!"

"What?" I said yet again. Joe's neck was flaming red, and I wondered if he was having an allergic reaction. The agitated blood vessels that were popping through his skin reminded me of raw hamburger meat. All I could envision was the chest-waxing scene with Steve Carell from the movie *40 Year-Old Virgin*. "Are you crazy, Suzanne?"

Poor Joe … But wait a minute … This could be fun, I thought as my sadistic side reared its evil head.

Welcome to the conception of our Whiskey and Waxing promotion. A shot of Gentleman Jack was offered first. Next the man in question enjoyed a relaxing shampoo and scalp massage that left his leg shaking like a dog. After the cut, however, his pleasure ended. The stylist quickly powdered his neck to absorb the moisture, rolled on the wax, and positioned the cloth strip. Within seconds he was squealing like a little girl. Sometimes we took extra delight in laboring a little longer on those men we knew were dogs.

"You're taking one for the team," I often joked. "We have to get bikini waxes for you. After all, it's your faces down there, not ours."

This promotion was short lived. Many of the brave souls who welcomed this idea at first changed their minds shortly after the experience. As for my stylist mind-set, this was payback to all the men who have left broken hearts scattered around the world.

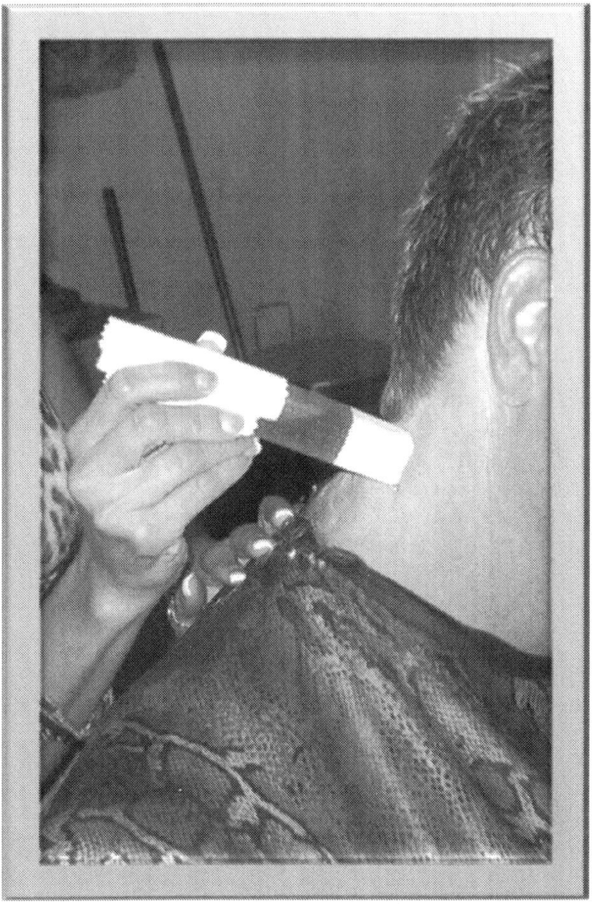

Whiskey and Waxing Promotion

Dan and Michael

Does size really matter? According to Dan, my first client of the day, it definitely does.

"Recently, I dated a girl who was only a B-cup," he said. "I can tell you with absolute certainty that if she had been more like a full C, I would have tolerated much more from her. I even made a comment about a friend I thought was really attractive because of her huge boobs, but her negative reaction made it clear that a little enhancement probably wasn't in the cards."

After that less-than-heartwarming story, I was glad when Michael, a prominent plastic surgeon, came in later that day. He was the perfect person to ask about the breast factor.

"I'm curious," I said. "What made you go into cosmetic surgery?"

"I was originally in pharmaceutical sales," he said, "and then recruited by a company that manufactured silicone breast implants. Driving to my first sales call, I palmed the samples, wondering if they felt like the real thing. I realized that I couldn't really tell, because it had been so long since I had touched a real one."

I couldn't hide my surprise at that rather odd comment. Luckily, before I could decide how to respond, he explained that his wife never liked him to touch her breasts.

"A few years and several sales later, a doctor invited me to sit in on a surgery," he continued. "I'm embarrassed to admit it, but when he let me feel the real breast and then the newly implanted one, I immediately got a full erection. I can't even remember if I felt a difference or not, but I do know that at that point, my life changed. Not because I'd touched another woman but because I learned later in the week that my wife had breast cancer."

"Oh no! How terrible!" I said, putting down my scissors to offer him my full attention. "Is she okay now?"

He nodded and said, "I was devastated, but tried to stay positive for her. I was beside her every step of the way, holding her hand as she suffered through the agonizing chemotherapy, the vomiting, the hair loss, and finally the mastectomy. With my encouragement, she eventually had both breasts removed and replaced with implants. I'm happy to say that today she is cancer-free and has a fabulous figure. As a bonus, we got to reconnect on many different levels, from our spiritual side to our sensual side."

"So that's when you decided to become a surgeon?" I asked.

"Yes. She persuaded me to finish my remaining three years of medical school, and now works in my office comforting women with similar stories."

If my day hadn't begun with Dan's off-putting anecdote about the power of a woman's breasts, I would never have heard the inspiration behind Michael's story.

Ed, Chris, and Rob

A client named Ed once said, "A perfect afternoon is lying on the couch with my pants unbuttoned, drinking a cold beer, and watching sports. It could be any kind of sporting event: baseball, football, auto racing. Heck, I'll even watch synchronized swimming if nothing else is on."

Chris, another client, argued, "All I need is to be fed, fucked, and left alone." His testicles must have been made of solid gold, because I can't imagine anyone saying something so bold, especially with shears that close to his jugular. He added, "Really, men have three basic needs: food in their stomach, possession of the remote, and lots of sex without warming the oven or cooling it down." Another client, Rob, overheard our conversation and interrupted, "Unless she wants to get up and grab me another beer."

Does testosterone really make the man? It's a debate that's been waged in scientific and social circles for decades. Some call it the hormone of desire. Testosterone is a potent androgenic hormone produced mainly by the testes, and is responsible for the development of male secondary sex characteristics. In 1889 Charles Edouard Brown-Sequard, a French psychologist, concocted a rejuvenating therapy for the body and mind. His elixir was a liquid extract made from the testicles of guinea pigs and dogs. Brown-Sequard claimed that this juice increased his physical strength and intellectual prowess, relieved his constipation, and increased the arc of his urine. Centuries before, in the quest for the Viagra of the ancients, testis tissue was the recommended fix for impotence.

Okay, but what about the obsession with the remote control? Why is it that he clings to that thing like a baby to a blanket? Men need to feel in charge, if only by means of a remote control. My client claimed *he* wore the pants in the family, but I know for a fact that *she* picked them out. Guys only need to think that they are in control.

What about directions and road maps? Is it a personal challenge or are they simply being idiots? They will drive around for hours knowing it is making us nuts. It all comes down to the control thing again. Men hate to admit they don't know what they're talking about. Allan Pease, coauthor of *Why Men Don't Listen and Women Can't Read Maps,* says that "men had to rely on spatial skills to survive. They needed to know where to throw the spear to hit the zebra running at high speeds, and how to get back home with the meat. So to have to stop and ask for directions is to admit you've failed at your number one evolutionary task!"

I laughed when a new client told me, "Sorry, I'm late! I couldn't find your salon."

"Did you put it in your GPS?"

"Uh, no. I knew I could figure it out."

They are always so proud of themselves. I never have the heart to remind them that if he had asked for directions, he would not have been ten minutes late. Men have a thirst for adventure that women just cannot curb, no matter how hard they try.

Accepting men for who they were created to be has been my biggest challenge. My mother used to wear a pin that I loved. It said, "When God made men, SHE was only kidding."

Remember

As they flex their muscles and stare at you through their testosterone-tinted glasses, keep in mind that this hormone is known to cause crown balding. So let those boys brag all about their testosterone. We know the truth!

Men who are bald at front of their heads
are good thinkers. Men who are bald at
the back of their heads are good lovers.
Men who are bald at front and
back think they are good lovers.
Hair today, gone tomorrow!

CHAPTER 3
Head Trips

A wise woman puts a grain of sugar into everything she says to a man, and takes a grain of salt with everything he says to her.
—Helen Rowland Sam

Exotic dancers understand the importance of giving men attention. After all, grabbing and holding the interest of their clients is what they depend on to bring home the bacon.

"After a head-banging day of work, my boys decided I needed a little TLC at the strip club," Sam said. "I hadn't had the chance to eat yet, so I immediately ordered a medium-rare steak. My mood slid downhill pretty fast, though. The steak was taking forever to come out, and my stomach was growling."

"I get that way when I'm hungry too," I agreed as I put the correct blade on the clippers.

"My buddies came up with the perfect solution to brighten my frame of mind. They bought me a lap dance," he said with a chuckle.

"Not a bad choice," I said. "Try to take your attention off your hunger ..."

"Exactly, but as soon as this gorgeous brunette approached to lead me into the back room, my dinner arrived," he said. "Now, that was a real dilemma. She was beautiful, but I was starving. A man has got to eat, so before going behind the curtain I motioned for my pal to hand me my plate. I sat down to watch the show and began to cut into this juicy piece of meat ..."

"How perfect! The best of both worlds," I joked.

"This was the most erotic dinner I have ever had. She ended up taking my fork and plate and feeding me bites while teasing me as she continued to shake her money maker. I'm not going to lie. It was the first time I ever got a hard-on while eating a steak!"

Now, that was one smart woman. Sprinkling a little motherly love on top of spicy hip thrusts made the perfect recipe. Word of advice: do try this at home! If you have just the right ingredients, your man will be more than satisfied.

"When I asked for a little off the top, I meant my hair ...but if you insist."

Larry

Larry was fifteen minutes late. While I waited, I noticed a face I didn't recognize in the stylist's chair beside mine. As the owner, I thought it was important to introduce myself, so I did. The man struck me as rather reserved, or maybe he was just quietly observing the salon since it was his first time visiting.

When Larry finally walked in, I glanced at the clock and said, "Hi, Lar. Since you're late, I only have fifteen minutes. I'll have time to cut you, but I probably won't have time to blow you."

The room, usually filled with chatter, suddenly fell silent. Immediately I realized my faux pas. It felt as if someone had pressed the slow-motion button as the words fell from my mouth. Larry's eyebrows rose, and a smile began cracking across his face. The stylist and the slightly aloof client next to me were both staring, eyes bulging and mouths open. Tongue-tied and at a loss for how to correct my wording, I prayed for someone to break the ice.

I wouldn't have predicted it, but it was the quiet new guy who saved the day.

"*I* was on time ...," he muttered.

Dr. Drew

"Looks like life has been good to you since I was last here," Dr. Drew said shortly after sitting down in my chair. "You've been hitting the white bread, I see."

"What do you mean by that?" I asked. Of course I already knew what he meant, but I couldn't entirely believe he would have the audacity to say it.

"Maybe it's the dress," he said, "but it looks like you've put on a few."

After I had given him the golden opportunity of silence to rethink his comment, he repeated it. Obviously he wasn't worried about how his haircut might turn out or the ear he might lose. Unbelievable. As I followed him to the shampoo bowl, I had to bite my tongue to keep from mentioning his own portly physique.

"So how have *you* been?" I asked to change the subject.

"I've been okay, but my wife isn't talking to me today," he said.

After his earlier comment to me, I didn't really need to question him, but I did for the sake of conversation. "Why? What did you do?"

"Nothing," he said with a chuckle. "I guess that's what's bothering her. She gave me a honey-do list before leaving for Chicago, and I was too busy to get much done."

Assuming his job as an ER surgeon had demanded his attention, I asked, "More patients than time these days?"

"No, I've been off all week," he said. "I played eighteen holes on Monday and another eighteen on Tuesday, and enjoyed a massage with the recommended nap on Wednesday. After that a buddy invited me on an overnight fishing expedition. I had previously committed to play in a charity scramble on Saturday, and then that evening I had to meet a guy at the Cigar Bar to discuss a new knee-brace product. Of course my weekly poker game was a necessity. I had to win back what I lost last week."

"Wow! I can see why you had no time," I said as I rolled my eyes.

Peter

Pete was an accountant, and he looked exactly like most people would picture: tall, reed-thin, with chronic dark circles around his eyes as though he had been up all night counting burlap bagfuls of Starbucks coffee beans. But even the tired and bloodshot eyes of an overworked CPA are drawn to a woman's bent-over form like a magnet to a refrigerator.

After coming in the first Wednesday of every month at two o'clock for as long as I could remember, Pete was trained to head straight to the shampoo station when I was ready for him. This particular day Suzanne was bent over the basin washing her client's hair. Since I was following behind him, I couldn't see what caused Pete to suddenly cut the corner short and run straight into the wall. Holding his aching forehead with his hand, he claimed he was fine when Suzanne turned around to ask. It wasn't until Pete passed that I noticed what had captivated his attention. The top of Suzanne's T-back panties was revealed as she rinsed, and she was oblivious to the whole thing.

"Caught ya," I said to Pete, snickering with one hand covering my mouth and the other shaped like an L on my forehead.

He begged me not to bring any more attention to it.

"Oh, Pete," I said, barely getting the words out between giggles. "That lump on your head says it all. I don't have to say a word. I'll leave it up to you to explain it to your wife."

"But did you see that?"
Only SISQO can phrase it the correct way,
"That Thong th thong thong thong..."

Andrew

"Another beer, Andrew?" I asked.

"No thanks," he said. "Another mirror!"

"Huh?"

"Another mirror would be great," he said again as he swiveled around in his chair to see the back of his head.

"That is not going to lie down, Andrew," I said. "Not even if you glob on the heaviest paste we have. Sorry, that's just the way your hair grows."

"It's a cowlick," he said.

"A cowlick?"

"Yeah, like when you were a baby and your mom licked her fingers to lay your hair down … You know … Maybe cows did it."

"I don't know where the name came from," I said, "but I do know that your growth pattern changes at your crown. That's why it sticks up. It doesn't know which direction to go."

"Can't you do something about it?" Andrew pleaded, pressing down on the offending piece of hair.

"I wish I could. Next time we'll leave it a bit longer and see if that helps."

"But what will I do in the meantime?"

"Put a little hairspray on it while it's still wet," I said.

This was a common conversation. With his full head of dark-brown hair and piercing blue eyes, Andrew was actually lucky.

As my mother always said, "Where there is hair, there is fun."

Give these guys a little pampering, and look out; we are suddenly fighting over the mirror!

For example, Al, a construction superintendent, was nice and polite at first. He would say, "Do whatever you think looks good."

Then after a time, he began to run me like he did his construction crew. "Hey, cut my hair a little shorter this time. It grew out way too fast. And don't forget to trim my eyebrows."

When had I ever forgotten to trim his eyebrows? He also wouldn't have had anything to worry about if he had maintained his routine of coming in every four to five weeks.

Eventually I learned not to waste my breath on challenging the clients. After all, I was the one who had spoiled them in the first place. I taught them and trained them to *look* like models, though, not to *act* like them. Telling me what to do and what products to use became almost an epidemic, as if they all met outside in the parking lot beforehand.

Then I discovered how to nip it in the bud by asking, "When did you get your license?"

"What?""So when did you get your license from cosmetology school? From the looks of you, I'd say you didn't finish." That became my way of stating my position as the stylist.

There is a lot to be said for a good haircut. A style can accent a jawbone or make a nose appear smaller. The handsome reflection in the mirror often catches a client's own eye. I never noticed how much men love themselves until I stepped behind the chair. Some are subtle about it, but others can sit and admire themselves for the entire thirty minutes. Some even enjoy watching their own expressions during conversation.

I realized I could use the mirror to my advantage. This basic piece of glass that cast one's reflection could expose their souls. It has been said that until you are twenty-five years old, you have the face you were born with. After that you have the one you deserve. Fortune-tellers claim they can read lines on people's faces and know where they've been. Before my reflective discovery, I would have called that crazy talk.

Talking to a man eye to eye could be somewhat uncomfortable, but when looking at his eyes in the reflection of the mirror, I felt like a spy watching every expression. From the seedy to the seductive, it became my own game of espionage.

Many times the newfound talent interfered with my casual conversation. If they were exaggerating or downright lying, I could almost read their thoughts. I knew which were tender, vulnerable, compassionate, and honest, and which were narcissistic sociopaths. Everyone has heard the cliché that if you hang out with someone long enough, that person begins to show his or her true colors. Examining those vibrant hues through the mirror told the story much more quickly.

I found that some men had ideas and desires so intricate and complex that I could get lost listening. Some were so contrived that I actually enjoyed being manipulated. Others were so comforting, gentle, and easy to talk to that it led to an insatiable craving. Sometimes I wished their hair grew faster!

CHAPTER 4
The Makeover

Women marry men hoping they will change.
Men marry women hoping they will not.
So each is inevitably disappointed.
—Albert Einstein

"Hey, cowgirl! What's with the new getup?" I asked Ashley after she sauntered into the salon wearing a ten-gallon hat.

Ashley, one of my stylists, usually exhibited first-rate fashion sense. At least she did until another guy waltzed into her life. Only months earlier she had showed up at work donned in a leather outfit, biker boots, and a fashion scarf. The warm leather jacket never left her body, since she wanted to stay true to her new image. Later we learned that she had met a guy at the cantina who drove a Harley-Davidson. She suddenly considered herself his "biker bitch" and proclaimed herself a motorcycle expert.

Shortly after the Harley guy rode off into the sunset without her, she came in wearing a floral dress laced up to her neck. That time her love interest was a born-again Christian, and, incredibly, she even considered becoming a Sunday school teacher at his church.

On this day when she rolled into the salon looking hotter than ever, wearing black lizard-skin cowboy boots, skin-tight jeans, a snug V-neck T-shirt that showed every bit of her voluptuous curvature, and a black belt with a buckle that looked like she had just taken first place at a national bull-riding championship, it wasn't hard to figure out the type of guy she was dating. He was a suburban "wannabe" cowboy.

"Just signed up for a step-dance class at Inn Cahoots," she said, apparently forgetting that she used to make fun of our local country bar at every opportunity.

Why do some women change their entire image with every new beau? I'll admit that it can be healthy to some extent, since everyone should try to broaden their knowledge and open their minds enough to attempt unfamiliar things. Experimentation is fun, but it isn't a good idea to give up your own originality and unique spirit. After all, that is what attracted him to you in the first place.

Keeping up a phony impression is also extremely tricky. The true you will always shine through eventually.

Glen

"How are things going with the new girlfriend, Glen?" I asked during an extremely busy day at the salon.

"Not so well. We broke up."

"Really? That's a shame. You seemed so into her the last time we talked," I said. "What happened?"

"When we met at a friend's house, she appeared to be the life of the party," Glen said. "The first four or five dates were a blast. We tried new restaurants, went hiking and biking, and did all sorts of other adventurous activities. We had so much in common in the beginning."

"So she changed?" I guessed as I ran a comb through his wavy auburn hair.

"Yeah. It was like someone suddenly turned off the lights," he said. "I don't know if it was because she figured she already had me hooked or what, but she began wearing sweats and watching reality shows every night."

"Kind of boring, right?" I asked. "How did you break up with her?"

"I began distancing myself little by little until I stopped calling her altogether. When she called me, I told her I was busy with a project." He laughed. "It wasn't a lie. I just didn't say that the project's name was Samantha."

Keith, another client, was sitting in Suzanne's chair next to Glen and chuckled. "I hear you, bro," he said. "At least you found out sooner rather than later."

"Uh oh," I said. Suzanne and I exchanged a knowing glance. We loved it when our clients shared stories with each other. Terrific entertainment.

"When I first met my wife," Keith said, "she was in stilettos. I haven't seen those in about twenty years."

Glen clapped his hands together. "Exactly!"

Both men laughed, enjoying their newfound comradeship.

"Her closet must have swallowed them," Keith said, "the same way she swallows every crumb in a bag of Oreo cookies."

"Ouch!" Suzanne and I said in unison.

"Don't get me wrong, girls," Keith said. "I still love her, but it's frustrating. She continues to blame the birth of our first son, who's now nineteen, for her swollen waistline. She gobbles up everything but the kitchen sink, and then is too embarrassed to go on our annual houseboat trip with our old college friends. She refuses to put on a bathing suit and won't make love to me unless she's been drinking."

"And women wonder why we don't stay satisfied," Glen added, shaking his head.

Brian

When I asked Brian, a conservative police officer, if he wanted the usual cut, he joked that he had always wanted to try a lime-green Mohawk.

"No one would know it was you at work, that's for sure," I said, trying to picture him wearing the punk-rock hairstyle with his uniform.

This led into a conversation about a recent wedding he had attended where he had run into his ex-wife and almost not recognized her.

"She didn't look anything like she did when I met her," he said. "We ended up divorcing when I refused to pay for her credit card debts. I already worked a full-time job and picked up side jobs when they were available, but it wasn't enough for her."

"What was she buying?" I asked. "Clothes and stuff?"

"Everything. She was never satisfied. A bigger house, a fancier car, a boob job, an extravagant trip. I simply couldn't keep up. The last I heard, she was dating a plastic surgeon and had a bunch of work done."

"She must have, if you almost didn't recognize her," I said.

"Yeah, her lips were huge and her breasts … well … you can imagine," he said. "We chatted for a few minutes, and she told me the plastic surgeon was out and the tattoo artist was in. She turned around to show me a huge cheetah inked across her back. I couldn't believe this was the same girl I used to know. I thought our marriage ended because I didn't make enough money, but apparently she had serious self-esteem issues from the beginning. Love is blind, as they say."

Wouldn't it be easier if you knew yourself first, so you could express the real you from the start? Brian's ex may have just needed more time to explore the many aspects of her personality before choosing a life partner. I wonder if she has figured it out yet.

These problems, of course, also happen in reverse. What about the woman who commits to a man with the sole intention of changing him once he says "I do"?

Tim

"Are you doing anything special this weekend, Tim?" I asked as I began to trim his sandy-brown hair.

"Yeah, unfortunately I have a wedding to attend," he said with an exaggerated sigh.

"Not a big fan of weddings, I take it?"

"It's not so much the event I dislike. It's more about another friend biting the dust."

I laughed and said, "It's not a funeral, Tim."

"Sometimes it feels like it. At first I was really happy for him. I thought that with a name like Lola, she would be an exciting addition to our group of friends—a perfect match for our group of misfits. Then the changes started. She's Mexican with a huge family, and she soon began conning him into attending another birthday party, baptism, reunion, or other family affair. Even when he manages an escape to play a quick game of golf, his phone never stops ringing. I can hear her whining and complaining from several feet away.

"And he puts up with that?" I asked.

"Yep, he's completely whipped. I'm left wondering how long a marriage can survive when it involves giving up every enjoyable aspect of your life. So let's say that I'm not exactly thrilled about the upcoming nuptials."

I was tempted to tell him that his friend should stand up and lay down some ground rules before it was too late. It appeared he was on the fast track to a complete loss of his man-card.

An older couple were lying in bed one night. The husband was falling asleep but the wife was in a romantic mood and wanted to talk. She said, "You used to hold my hand when we were courting." Wearily he reached across, held her hand for a second and tried to get back to sleep. A few moments later she said, "Then you used to kiss me." Mildly irritated, he reached across, gave her a peck on the cheek and settled down to sleep. Thirty seconds later she said, "Then you used to bite my neck." Angrily, he threw back the bed clothes and got out of bed. "Where are you going?" she asked. "To get my teeth!"

CHAPTER 5

Does Your Carpet Match Your Drapes?

First, I'm going to start dyeing my eyebrows, just to see how it works. And then I'll go to the hair. Start slowly.
—George Clooney

Why is it that the day you decide not to wear makeup is the day you run into your mate's ex? She looks like a million bucks, whereas you look like you just crawled out of a cave. Interestingly enough, this has happened to almost all of us at one point or another.

Strap on a pair of sexy stilettos and come to work with me. Let's listen to what my clients say about women's grooming. Before we go, observe that I am wearing a low-cut shirt and push-up bra. Believe it or not, this is on account of my ex-husband's advice.

"Give those guys a little something extra today," he said on more than one occasion. "They'll love it."

Many men would stop their wives at the door if they tried that. When I took his advice, though, I noticed a definite difference in tips by the end of the day. My clients showed their appreciation and paid for their delight. Maybe my ex-husband was just fond of the larger gratuities I brought home, but he certainly knew what guys liked.

I used to worry about exposing too much, and didn't want to appear starved for attention. Eventually I was hit with a realization: I was proud of the way my tactfully clad cleavage looked, so how could I fault a man who was only expressing his approval?

Okay, let's not keep the clients waiting any longer…

"If it's a Saturday morning and my girlfriend and I are just running errands, I don't see the need for makeup," William, my ten o'clock, said. "She is so naturally beautiful that it's a shame to cover it up."

"Hmm … interesting," I said, glancing at Brandon, my odd-jobs man, who was working on the salon's decorative fountain.

"Don't get me wrong," William added. "There is a time and place for the fancy face and hair, but for a casual weekend you should just enjoy the freedom we guys have."

"Just go naked, huh?" I asked.

"Did I hear the word *naked*?" Brandon said with a snort as he walked up to my station.

I turned around and laughed. "Yes, you did. How long do you think the fountain will stay in working condition this time?"

"Should last a little while this time," he said. "Just try to keep it clean. While I'm here, Stacie, do you think you could give me a quick trim?"

I glanced at my watch and said, "Sure. Have a seat. I'm almost finished with William here. Do you think I should be putting anything special in the water to keep the fountain clean?"

Brandon plopped down in the chair at the empty station next to mine and said, "You could try using distilled water to prevent mineral buildup, but the main thing is keeping the hair out of it."

"Easier said than done," I said, handing William a mirror and spinning him around in the chair.

William nodded his approval and said, "Looks good, Stacie."

"Okay, let's get you checked out. Be right back, Brandon. You can move over to this seat as soon as Angie sweeps up."

When I returned a couple of minutes later, Brandon was chuckling to himself. He said, "I was just remembering one of my ex-girlfriends, thanks to your fountain.

Her name was Jessica, but I secretly called her Messy Jessie."

"Wow! Not nice, Brandon," I said. "Come on back to the shampoo bowl."

"The entire time we lived together, our bathroom was covered with long red hair," he continued as we walked to the back of the salon. "All over the floor, in the sink, and clogging the shower drain. As a matter of fact, the whole house was a pigsty. I'm not the most organized person in the world, and I didn't expect her to be either. She was out of control though. I always thought women were naturally neat."

"No way!" I said as I adjusted the water temperature. "When I was a flight attendant, my hotel room always looked like a tornado aftermath. Although, in my defense, this was partly because I could never decide what to pack. The boots I wore in New York City wouldn't be appropriate in a Madison, Wisconsin, bar, and the coat I bought in Rome wouldn't work in the Miami heat. Bag-dragging half of my wardrobe around the world became commonplace. Now that I'm grounded in one city, my tidy guy made it clear from the start that those habits weren't going to roll."

"Good for him," Brandon said as I toweled his hair dry. "I wouldn't say it was the main reason Jessica and I broke up, but it definitely didn't help. It seemed odd that for such a slob, she took really good care of her body. She showered twice a day and smelled great. Her toenails were always painted pretty colors, and I know she shaved, because she had these gorgeous, smooth legs that drove me wild."

"So you're not into the hairy, au naturel, or 'wookie' look, then?" I teased.

Catching on to my underlying meaning, he replied, "Oh, I definitely prefer a nice landing strip to the sixties fur coat, just as long as the carpet matches the drapes."

If you think "manscaping" means mowing the lawn around your mailbox only to make it look taller, I have news. True manscaping involves the whole package. Dave, a divorced real estate agent, often joked about his being the tallest mailbox in the neighborhood. After I'd asked whether his girlfriend appreciated his fine grooming, our comic banter suddenly shifted back to business.

"More people than you would imagine make an offer on a home before ever walking inside, simply judging by the landscaping," he said. "It's called curb appeal."

This is something many women do in relationships. Based on appearance alone, women fall heart first. The way a guy looks and dresses, as well as the car and home he owns, sends women racing to the bridal shop. Meshing her first name with his last and stocking up on glossy wedding magazines after knowing only his outward appearance is dangerous. It is a recipe for certain failure, yet many are surprised when the relationship lasts only a short time.

With his clients, Dave insists on an inside home tour. "More women should take the same tour when meeting a man," he added.

The challenge is getting through the narrow entryway of the front door and looking around. If you devote the time and don't get sidetracked, you will be rewarded with a glimpse of his true self … the essence of *him-ness.*

The rooms in a home resemble the unique personalities that reside within its occupant. The foyer is usually what he wants you to see. The living room is rarely used, and is therefore often a staged façade with generic art on the walls, an uncomfortable sofa, and dust on the tables if he does not have a maid.

Move into the family room. This is where you will gain the most perspective about who he is. It is where he spends the majority of his time when he's not with you. What do you find there? Is it cluttered or clean? Is there an oversized flat screen on the wall or a 1960s wood-framed stand-alone? This may show how freely he spends his money. Is there a worn spot on the sofa, signaling a possible coach potato, or a treadmill and weights? How about family pictures?

Next on the tour is his bedroom. Is it inviting, or does it appear barren? Do you notice neat, hospital-style corners on his bed or Spider-Man sheets in disarray? Are there candles on the dresser? How much have they been burned? This will tell you if there have been other recent visitors. The kitchen is where you can determine if he cooks, overeats, does the dishes, or expects you to. The contents of the refrigerator will also reveal quite a lot of information. Moldy Chinese take-out containers and beer may be typical for a single guy without culinary aspirations, but what about Cap'n Crunch and chocolate milk?

Inching my way to the front to trim and texture his bangs, I had to ask, "How do you know all this, Dave?"

His answer was simple. "It's common sense!"

He had a point, so I asked him to continue.

"Don't look in his garage until you're serious about him," he said. "It's none of your business. And if you haven't come to a conclusion by the time you've experienced his inside living conditions, then you need to spend more time with him."

Jim, a client seated next to him, chimed in with, "How he treats his car, boat, or motorcycle is most likely how he is going to treat you."

As I reached for my blow dryer, my next appointment, seated in a wing-backed chair, interjected, "But I'll warn you, if he has a dog, he may treat that dog better!"

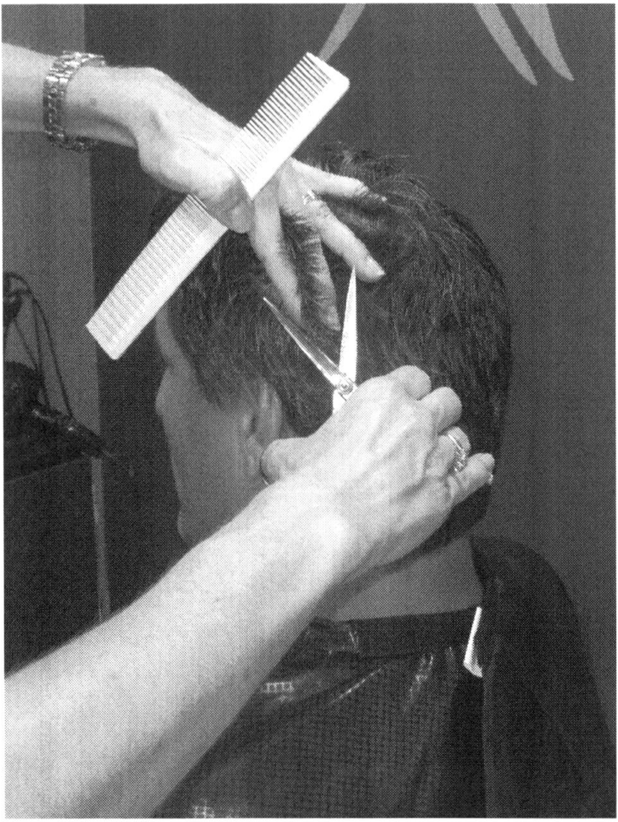

CHAPTER 6
Rock Paper Scissors

"Love is like war: easy to begin but very hard to stop."
-H. L. Menchen

Day after day I stood behind my chair listening as my clients divulged their opinions on relationships. They would even offer advice on how men process thoughts. Even though I took it all in, soaking up every word, I'm still a woman and I fall for the same things other would women do. After my first serious relationship failed, I had a difficult time finding a man perfect for me. Like most women, I made quick judgments based solely on first impressions. For example, I jumped into relationships faster than I could jump on the back of a Harley Davidson just because the rider had tribal tattoos and a bad-ass bike, another spoke with an Australian accent and could sing and play guitar, before I could blink an eye, I was sitting stage side at all his performances. Don't get me wrong, I was in love both times but it was not the kind of love that would quench my insatiable desire to seek something deeper. I searched for one who would indulge me, keep me entertained, and yet let me be me. Most of the ones I found fell short of my expectations, especially since I was looking for qualities I didn't possess myself.

At the age of thirty-one, I, as many in their thirties do, embarked on a soul-searching journey. I spent the majority of that year with my golden retriever, Clyde. Together, we hiked, hit the beach, and marveled at sunsets. Instead of entertaining the idea of "this guy may be the one," I took the time to define my personal goals and began a quest to learn who I was. I took a closer look at my desires and accomplishments. I dug deep and proudly came to this conclusion, instead of morphing into a man's lifestyle, I realized it was going to take quite the man to intertwine with mine.

That same year I lost a close male friend to cancer. Being so young, I never imagined the disease would attack one of my very own. As a way to cope with the grief, I set out to host a cut-athon in my friend's name to benefit the American Cancer Society. This proved to be a powerful distraction. Suddenly there was no room in my mind for the fact that I was single. Within one week of hosting the event, unbelievably, I met the man who would soon sweep me completely off my feet.

Still feeling high from pulling off such a lofty endeavor, I went out with friends one evening, and there he stood—all six feet five inches of him. He had eyes of blue and a body so strong and muscular that I would gladly have paid him just to come over and fish a leaf out of my pool. One glance and I was giddy, we talked for hours that night but it was what happened the next day that hooked me. Chatting with a mutual friend, I wanted to know everything about my new crush. When I mentioned his name, my friend said, "You mean Scott Harmon, the champion—"

That was all it took before I stopped listening and immediately began nodding in agreement. "Sure, that sounds great," I said, already envisioning my savior riding in on his milky-white steed.

It didn't matter that the final word was *kickboxer*. *Champion kickboxer*. For all I cared, my friend could have said, "champion bug-killer for the local pesticide company." Like a damsel in distress peering down from a dragon-guarded tower, I set my sights on a knight.

I knew what it took to be a champion: dedication, devotion, perseverance, and pride. Those were the same hard-to-find qualities I was seeking in a man, and the reason I stayed single until the age of thirty-three.

Were we a match? Our schedules were not, as he was an early bird and I was a morning snoozer. He was somewhat of an introvert, whereas I was an extra-extrovert. He enjoyed gourmet cooking and landscaping, whereas I couldn't be bothered with mundane domestic activities. The world was my oyster and I wanted to find the pearl.

After two years of appreciating our differences, we married. Our wedding day was everything I had dreamed it should be. Our two week Grecian honeymoon was nothing short of blissful lovemaking and promises made to each other as the sun set over the island of Santorini. The first two years were full of love and new adventures but no one warned us about marital pressure and the required work from both of us to sustain a marriage. Coming from divorced families caused us both to have stronger values based on what we witnessed growing up. This armed us with thoughts that we were ready for the long haul. When I gave birth to our daughter, he gave birth to a new career. One would hold us together, but the other would tear us apart.

We sought marriage counseling. Our "coach" asked us what had attracted us to each other. My answer was simple: he was a champion. Scott's tall, muscular build and scarred face showed me that he could protect me, but I had never anticipated the sting the left jab of divorce would leave on my heart.

We often miss important signs in the beginnings of relationships. At first, I didn't realize how much Scott needed to win. From the smallest discussion to the biggest argument, there was simply no middle ground. He had to be victorious, but winning at all costs is not always worth the sacrifice.

Some women marry men believing they can transform or enhance them, like they would a house. This rarely works. A man may change for a little while, if he is smitten or feels he has something to gain from it, but it isn't long before he settles in and returns to those unattractive habits he possessed when you met.

I knew Scott was reckless before I married him; in fact, that intrigued me. Once we had a child, though, I changed. I was not as adventurous, as free-spirited, or as loving toward him. I worried about finances and needed more peace of mind. I was bossy, emotional, and hormonal. In short, I stopped being the girlfriend he had fallen in love with. I lost my balance.

The purpose for sharing my personal story of defeat is to remind you that we all make decisions that do not turn out the way we expect, however, the adventure is what we yearn for, so when it comes to men, I challenge you to have a sense of humor, a sense of adventure and to enjoy the ride. My hat goes off to all of those who have had the mental and emotional fortitude to keep their marriages alive and healthy.

Eighteen

A 54 year old mathematician left his wife a note that said, "When you get this message, I'll be at the Grand Hotel with my 18 year old secretary."

The wife faxed him at the hotel with the following message, "When you get this your 54 year old wife will be at home with an 18 year old boy toy. Being a mathematician you know that 18 will go into 54 a whole lot more than 54 will go into 18."

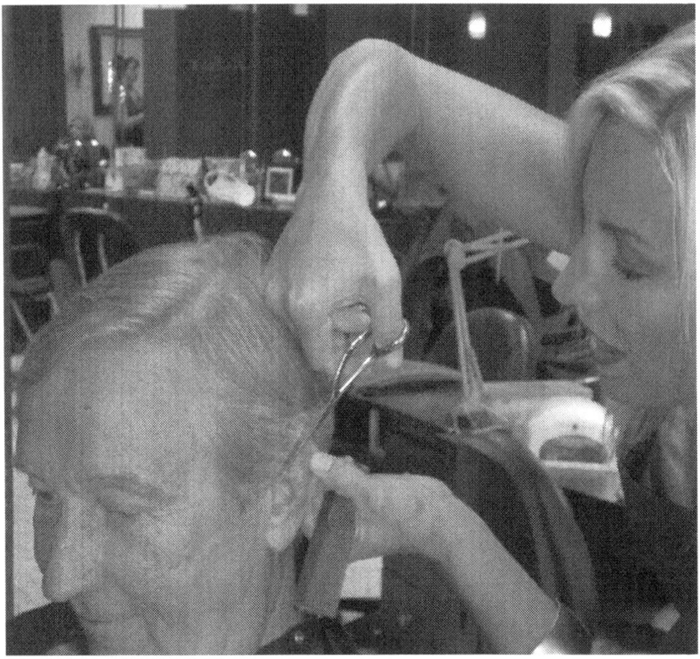

CHAPTER 7
Crown of the Matter

"When a young man complains that a young lady has no heart, it's pretty certain that she has his."
-George Dennison Prentice

Earl

My client Earl was the most sincere and loving man who has ever blessed my chair. Not only did he speak highly of his wife of sixty-three years, but he held her up on the pedestal he had put her on the day he married her.

One of my saddest days behind the chair was the day he buried her. I knew why he was getting his hair trimmed a week earlier than his regularly scheduled appointment, and the spray of the water was the only sound during his shampoo. At my station, however, he held on to every bit of strength he had at eighty-six years old, and told me their love story.

"She was a cashier at the local general store. I can't tell you how many unnecessary items I purchased," he said with a chuckle. "She was my sunshine, the first thing I wanted to see in the morning and the last at the end of every day. Never imagined she would take a liking to me, a simple car mechanic."

"But she must have," I said as I ran a comb through his sparse gray hair.

"There was an unexplainable attraction between us that she hid better than I did," he said. "Her smile lit up the room, but I thought that was just a necessary part of her job. Then one day she asked me if I wanted to share a malt from the ice cream shop next door. It felt as if I had won the lottery."

The memory must have struck a raw nerve within Earl. He paused for a moment with his head down, so I squeezed his shoulder in what I hoped was a comforting gesture. He raised his eyes to mine in the mirror and nodded, returning to the present.

"We shared that malt, all right, and I realized her smile had been genuinely for me. We had a connection," he said. "A person doesn't have to be a looker to everyone, only to you. There has to be a connection, and that connection better be strong. Life throws you curveballs that are tough to endure, unless you have someone or something to want to wake up for."

I finished up his hair with a touch of hairspray as I let his advice sink in. Wanting his story to continue, I had a hard time pulling off the cape and letting him go. This was the first time that Earl had ever shared his story of their courtship.

As he stood up and pulled out his wallet, I could hardly speak. I tapped his wallet and said with a cracking voice, "Today, it's on the house, Earl. I'm so sorry for your loss."

I could feel the emptiness he was experiencing as I hugged him goodbye. A teardrop streamed down my cheek as I told him to be strong. "This is one of those curveballs, Earl," I said.

He winked and gave me a partial smile before tightening his lips and walking out the door.

Joel

Joel, a connoisseur of fine gems, had owned his jewelry store for more than fourteen years—about the same amount of time he had been seeing his girlfriend, Nancy. Joel was married to Michelle, a stay-at-home mother tending to their four children, and Nancy's husband owned the car dealership down the street. During the time I spent styling Joel's silky strands, he described his complex relationship status.

"I first met Nancy at her husband's dealership when I bought my car," he confessed. "I hit it off with Nancy and her husband immediately. We started doing things together as couples and all became close friends. Michelle, my wife, is usually too tired to accompany me to different business and social events, so I soon found myself gravitating toward Nancy and her husband at those functions when I was flying solo. Even though I never expected to be so attracted to her, I quickly realized we had much in common."

Always curious about why a man would stray, I asked him to tell me more about the attraction.

He said, "Nancy's smile is always so genuine."

Knowing both couples, I felt the need to comment. "Well, with tending to four rather than two children like Nancy, whose smile wouldn't be a little forced at times?"

"I guess," he answered with a quick shrug, "but Michelle has become so boring that I rarely even ask about her day anymore. She will go on and on about toting the kids from here to there, with no sense of appreciation that she does so in a fully loaded SUV. Nancy is more appreciative and full of zest for life."

"Hmm ... okay," I said, putting the guard on my razor.

"Not to mention how she looks these days. After our first child was born, Michelle cut off her beautiful mane of red hair and became ... matronly. I hate to use that word, but that's what it is. If I say anything about it, she barks, 'It's all about easy right now, Joel. I hardly have time to comb it in the morning.' Nancy, as you know, always looks great, even when her gorgeous hair is pulled back in a pony."

"Both women are beautiful in their own way, Joel," I said democratically as I finished up his cut. "Do your spouses know about the affair?"

"I would be surprised if they didn't, since it seems so obvious to me. Most of the diamonds Nancy wears I gave her."

I forced a polite laugh, but couldn't help thinking how disrespectful that seemed.

Joel must have read my mind, because he said, "I suppose I lost respect for my wife a long time ago when she began to cut me down all the time. One night we were out with a few other couples, and she insulted me in front of everyone. That's when I noticed the compassion in Nancy's eyes, and I knew I was with the wrong woman. Now I'm stuck between a rock and a hard place. I long to be with Nancy, but I have an obligation to my wife."

From that day on I would often have to ask Joel, "Wait. Who are we talking about here? Your wife or your girlfriend?"

Keeping them straight was always a challenge, but thanks to his eye-opening opinion, the decision about whether to cut my hair in an easier-to-manage style was simple.

Brock

"Did you say PIG?" I asked again.

"Yeah, that's what we called it," Brock, a good-looking college graduate, said with a confident nod.

Seeing my shocked expression in the reflection of the mirror, he shrugged his broad shoulders. Perhaps coaching and steering as the coxswain on his college rowing team made it easy for him to coax his pals into doing something so belittling to women.

Now a high-end stockbroker, Brock admitted that what had started as a random event eventually turned into a monthly novelty with the guys.

"So how exactly did all of this start?" I asked, running a comb through his damp hair.

"Well, we would all cruise off campus and head to the next city," he answered, lowering his voice as another stylist and her client passed behind us on their way to the sinks. "The first goal of the competition was to dance with the largest girl in the place, and I'm not talking tall here."

"Nice." My comment dripped with sarcasm, but Brock didn't miss a beat.

"Whoever took the big girl home would win free drinks the next night the guys went out," he continued. "At the time it seemed completely harmless. The girls had no idea it was a joke, so they went home feeling happy and confident."

"Yeah, while you guys probably drove home making jokes and cracking up," I scolded.

Brock confessed that although he eventually realized the activity was cruel, it didn't stop him from trying to justify it. "Believe it or not, most of those friends are now married to heavyset women. Maybe I'm somehow responsible for that?"

I knew one of the guys Brock had mentioned in his story, so when Will came in for his monthly cut, I confronted him. He was horrified that I knew about the game. In defense, he shared his story with me.

"One night I was the one who went home with the girl," he began.

"You mean, the pig?" I interrupted.

"Yeah, I guess ...," he continued.

With slight satisfaction, I noticed a pink flush creeping up the back of his neck.

"But she really wasn't that big," he quickly added. "And her smile lit up the room. I ended up discovering that not only was she fun, but we had a lot in common. She made me dinner that night with whatever was in her fridge, and the pasta dish she whipped up beat any I've ever had in Little Italy. We spent the rest of the evening cuddled on the couch with a movie. I enjoyed her company so much that I forgot the original reason I went there."

"Aww," I said, feeling my indignation melting away. "What did you tell the guys?"

"When my cab pulled up at the frat house later that night, of course the guys were quick to heckle me. I managed to blow them off and call her later that day. For over a month I hid our relationship, spending a crapload of money on cab fare."

"Oh my God. Did they ever find out?"

"Yes. A few months later our college was playing the rival university. Everyone was hyped for this big day in football history. Without hesitation I called and invited her to Quarters, a sports bar that charged college students seventy-five cents a beer. After she accepted, I became concerned about how the guys were going to react. I was especially worried that they would tell her about the pig parties."

"Well, yeah. That would be a quick road to Dumpsville," I said, rubbing styling gel into his new cut. "So, did you get away with it?"

"Fortunately, she brought two smokin' hot friends," he said. "So the guys never said a word. Coincidentally, those four guys were in our wedding two years later."

"Did she ever find out about the parties?" I asked, handing him a mirror and spinning the chair around.

"No, thank God," he said while admiring his reflection.

Knowing Will's secret was a privilege, and it made me see him in a new light. Although I didn't condone his actions, I was glad he had discovered that he shouldn't judge a book by its cover.

CHAPTER 8
Blade o' Glory

A pessimist is a man who thinks all women are bad.
An optimist is a man who hopes they are.
--Chauncey Mitchell Depew

"I don't know what it is about that girl," Bob said, shaking his head in wonderment.

During Bob's appointments, the conversation always revolved around his crush on Jennifer, a coworker.

"I can't stop torturing myself," he continued. "She leads me on and then quickly reminds me that we're just friends. Is it game?"

"I don't know," I said. "What exactly does she do?"

"At work it's business as usual, but she's all over me when we join colleagues for drinks after work."

"It sounds like you want her so badly that you're missing some obvious information. She's more relaxed after a little alcohol," I pointed out. "Have you ever asked her on a date?"

"Yeah—check this out. Last month she gave me two tickets to a hockey game and then declined when I asked her to join me. Why would she give me two tickets if she didn't plan to go along?"

I shrugged, not entirely seeing his point. Hockey tickets sounded like the ideal gift for a guy, especially when she didn't expect him to ask her along.

A few months passed, and Bob continued to dissect his relationship with Jennifer when visiting the salon.

And then, "You won't believe it!" he said one day, kicking back in the shampoo chair. "One of my fellow insurance adjusters got married this past weekend, and guess who I had to sit next to?"

"Let me guess … Jennifer?" I said, teasing him.

"Guess again: Jennifer's fiancé."

"What?" I gasped in disbelief.

"That's right. This girl threw my heart into a blender and served it back to me as a smoothie. She never told me she had a boyfriend, let alone a fiancé."

"Guess you no longer have to fret over where you stand with her," I joked.

Jeff

"The Ring of Fire" is what he called it. Jeff, a project manager for a commercial building empire, scored a date with the woman of his dreams just before he came in for a haircut. I listened while he had a solo brainstorming session on unforgettable first-date ideas. With each snip of my silver shears, a new plan emerged from his lips. Since

Jeff taught surf lessons as a weekend side job, I suggested he teach her how to ride the waves. He quickly brushed off my idea, focusing on something bigger and brighter.

When he settled on a plan to head out to the beach beforehand, I was captivated. A picture of a candlelit table on the sand, gourmet cuisine served by a waiter in all black with a white linen towel over his left forearm, and a musician softly playing love songs in the background formed in my mind. The elegant image I had conjured up rapidly dissolved when he blindsided me with something that was more intense—or in my mind, INSANE.

Preparation involved hitting the beach early with a can of gasoline and a creative idea—or at least that's what Jeff thought. I was snipping away while listening, and all I could think was that nothing good could come from any idea involving gasoline, but I stayed quiet. Jeff's goal was to create the most memorable first kiss ever. He had a secluded spot on the beach in mind to execute his perfect plan. He was going to arrive earlier in the day and pour the gasoline in a twenty-foot circle. During the date, he planned to suggest a moonlit walk on the beach. When they arrived at the special spot, he would lay her down in the sand where their first kiss would be ignited, literally.

"I'm not sure I get it, Jeff," I said.

"Once I lay her back, I'll reach out to the circle and light it."

"Sounds a bit dangerous to me, but whatever turns you on."

His excitement was so infectious that I couldn't wait for him to come back so I could ask how it went.

"Well??? I'm dying to know. Did it work?" I asked during his next visit.

"Oh, it worked all right," Jeff said in a sarcastic tone. "It really lit her up. Let's just say that I should have made the circle thirty feet instead of twenty."

"What happened?" I asked, already cringing at the possible scenarios.

He had anticipated a slow, steady circle of fire, with flames flickering only one or two feet high. What he got was a roaring wall of fire that would have been the pride of any king from the Middle Ages who was trying to overthrow another kingdom by burning them out. It went so fast and so high that Jeff's date thought they had been bombed.

"As I was still trying to retrieve the romantic moment I had pictured in my mind, I felt I still needed to perform that first kiss. I was going to make it happen, because I was on a mission. I tried to kiss her after her panic attack, but all I can remember is the taste of salt; both of our faces were covered with sweat because of the ungodly temperatures surrounding us. It wasn't really romantic. Just then, I realized that I had also accidentally dribbled some gas inside the circle, so we had to do some sort of impromptu Native American sand dance to keep our shoes from catching fire."

"Oh my God! Jeff!" I said, unable to contain my shocked laughter. "I'm sorry!"

"That's okay. It's now a running joke that our first date was full of dinner, dancing, and a little fireside chat."

"So, you've gone out again?" I asked, surprised.

"As a matter of fact she now has a toothbrush and drawer at my house, not to mention her own garage space and garage-door opener after I moved the gasoline cans. So, yes, things are going really well. I must have gotten an A for effort!" It didn't hurt either that I bought her some eye pencils and mascara to help cover up all the singes.

So now, Jeff will always be known as the Ring of Fire.

Like is like a penis, simple, soft, and relaxed … its women that make it hard.

CHAPTER 9
Finishing Touches

If you want your dreams to come true, don't oversleep.
—Yiddish Proverb

He holds my head in his hands. I feel the rich aromatherapy oil seeping through to my roots. His fingers, rough with calluses, entangle my fragile hair. I'm aroused by the slight pain of the pull. I feel the warmth of his breath, still scented with Pinot Noir, on my forehead as he exhales. I imagine the flex of his biceps as he leans in and lifts my head, reaching for the nape of my neck. Gently, I touch my lips to his bare chest. Of its own accord my back arches as he whispers in my ear …

"Get up … get on up … Stay on the scene," James Brown demanded.

Bleary-eyed, I reached for my cell phone, trying to turn off the obnoxious alarm. After lying there for a few minutes with my eyes closed, I finally realized the futility of trying to pick up where I had left off. Why was that possible only with nightmares?

After donning my leopard-print robe and matching slippers, I stumbled down the hall to the kitchen. Instead of being greeted with the enticing aroma of coffee, however, an empty carafe gleamed coldly at me from the counter. Realizing that I had forgotten to set the timer, I mentally thanked God for Starbucks.

With my iced double-shot skinny vanilla latte in hand, I raced by the front desk of LA Fitness, barely stopping as I scanned my membership card. Scanning the scenery for eye-candy on my way to the locker room, I spotted him on the treadmill. The guy in my dream. His locks of dark, wavy hair moist with sweat from his sprint.

Making a quick decision, I set my latte down on a machine to frantically dig through my gym bag.

Sweet! I found one! I said to myself as I located one of my business cards. Even though it was slightly bent at the corners, I thought it would work. Luckily, scouting new clients was part of my job. This allowed me to boldly approach him and hand him the card. Without waiting for a reaction, I headed back to pick up my coffee. Before proceeding to the locker room, I couldn't resist a quick look back. I was delighted to find a raised eyebrow, a curled bottom lip, and a nod. A quick smile and I jetted on my way with confidence. *He'll call.*

Minutes later I watched him through the glass as he moved to the free weights. I couldn't stop staring until my no-holds-barred kickboxing instructor, Grant, moved in front of me, shouting, "Jab! Sidekick! Upper cut!"

A month passed, leaving the cutie on the treadmill almost forgotten. When he finally called, his deep voice on the other end of the line assured me that he had wanted to call sooner. Haircuts, though, were not high on his priority list since he preferred his hair on the longer side.

"Do you have any openings this afternoon?" he asked.

I skimmed my book for an open slot, but no luck. Not wanting to miss this opportunity, however, I took a moment to review my list of clients. Who was consistently late? Aha. My four o'clock was always lagging.

"Perfect. I'll see you then," he said.

Men pay attention far more than we give them credit for. At the gym that day, he had noticed that I was sipping something from a cup with a very recognizable logo. At 4:02, that cutie walked in with a caffé mocha from Starbucks.

Knowing he had brought the smile to my face made him keep coming back.

Men genuinely want to make us happy. They also want … freedom. Personal space is extremely important to them, but a man wants a woman who is genuinely game to try new things and accompany him in his interests. Someone who inspires him, makes him laugh with her youthful exuberance, and entices his hunger with her sultry side.

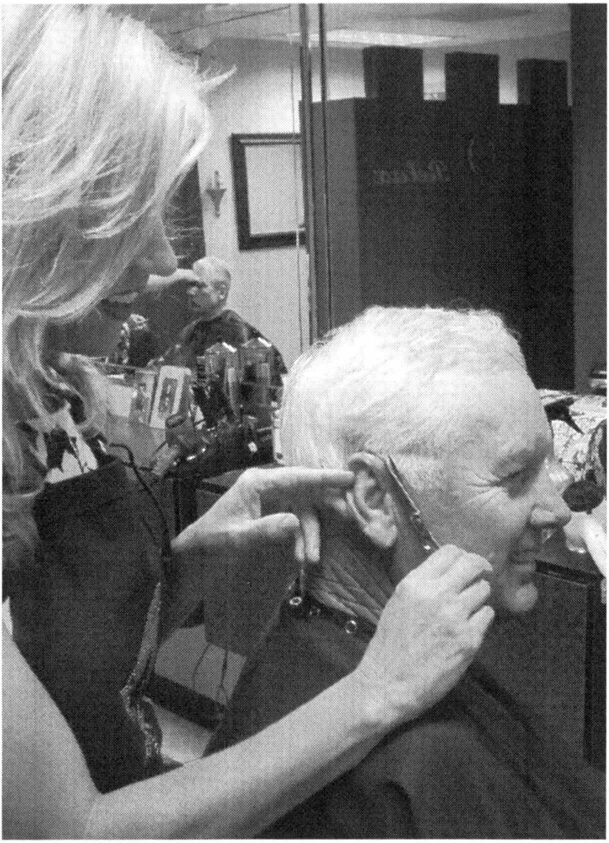

John

John, the local sheriff, had me feeling like I was handcuffed to the back of the chair when he began interrogating me. He had an uncanny way of asking questions without revealing that he was dissecting every response.

I was used to being the one who asked my clients the questions, so he caught me off guard when he turned to me and asked, "So, you're a beautiful girl. What are you looking for in a man?"

Baffled by his boldness, I thought for a minute and then stuttered, "I guess I want what every other woman wants. The obvious: a man who is loyal, handsome, loving, and devoted. Intelligent, charismatic, business-minded, body conscious, honest, witty, compassionate, balanced, considerate, athletic, sexy, adventurous, mechanical, and resourceful. Oh, and certainly one who doesn't do drugs, smoke, drink, or gamble excessively. I guess that about covers it," I said, reaching for my thinning shears.

"Huh. That is exactly what men look for in women," he replied.

It all made sense. Be the kind of person you would like to find. Don't expect to find characteristics in someone else that you don't possess yourself. I made that mistake with the man who became my husband. I was smitten because he possessed characteristics that I did not.

He was grounded and owned his own business, and I was a free-spirited flight attendant gallivanting around the world. He had savings, and I lived paycheck to paycheck. He could build anything, such as my walk-in closet and kitchen pantry, and could even cook. The problem was that because he was willing and capable, I expected him to do the majority of these things instead of challenging myself. This lack of balance caused him to grow resentful.

At one point we tried role reversal, because of a new job that provided him more freedom. He became more free-spirited, footloose, and fancy-free, leaving me to manage the household, pay the bills, make dinner, juggle my job, and care for our child. It wasn't long until I transformed into the resentful one.

Sadly, after our divorce, I discovered that I enjoyed cooking, cleaning, and gardening. Managing my home, child, and career gave me a sense of empowerment. If I had stepped out and tried these things before, I may not have had to feel the devastation of divorce.

According to what I learned from my clients, like-mindedness, compatibility, and balance seem to be the key to a fulfilling relationship. For example, if you are not financially savvy, don't expect to marry a man with money just to be taken care of. He will resent it in the long run. Get out there and become financially secure on your own; it's so much more attractive to a man. If you're looking for a man who is physically fit, you may need to lose those twenty extra pounds and adjust your eating habits. Perhaps you're searching for a charitable go-getter? Join a local volunteer group or spearhead a fund-raiser. One client in particular had this to say: "Find simple things that enrich your own life, and he will take notice."

Expectation can be the enemy.

Highly explosive, expectations can blow a relationship to pieces before it ever gets off the ground. Many women set their expectations so high that even a pole-vaulter couldn't elevate himself to that height.

Knowing the salon was full of solid and successful men, my single girlfriends were invariably asking me to introduce them to someone fabulous. Although it's true that there is no shortage of desirable suitors, I couldn't bring myself to throw any one of my clients to the proverbial wolves. I knew all too well those women's insatiable expectations and their insidious behaviors of the past. One overweight friend wanted a man with a six-pack, and another expected a man to take her and her five kids to dinner every night. Another was looking for a man (any man) to support her so she could quit her dreaded job. The list was endless.

I have to confess that when I first picked up my laptop and began this adventure in writing, I had a very different view of men. After just a year of shampooing and shearing, I was certain I could pick each client apart and categorize him. To my surprise, my research and discoveries taught me that there is no category for many of them. I learned more than I ever imagined, especially about myself.

I originally wanted an unpredictable man who could hold my interest and make my heart race. Although someone who has the ability to entice and excite me is still desirable, I'm now more intrigued by a man who can also provide emotional and financial security. One who makes me feel I can achieve anything purely because of who I am. One who can shoulder my many moods and even think it's cute when I'm being headstrong and stubborn. Someone who adjusts his own expectations because he sees my favorable qualities, which to him outweigh those that are less appealing.

One of my all-time favorite clients often reminds me, "Marry first for romance, second for finance." He has a point. Life becomes more financially challenging. When we are young, we can appreciate living on a dime, but as our taste for the finer things becomes more robust, so does the price.

Many women claim they are anti-drama, yet sit in my chair and burden me with their minutiae. They are so caught up in how men never measure up that it exhausts me to listen. I do not share their views. As time has matured my opinions, I have adjusted my expectations. Notice that I use the word *adjusted* as opposed to *lowered* or *raised.* I believe the magic word is *adjusted.* Adjustment is crucial for a relationship to flourish. As Earl said, life throws us curveballs, and we have to learn how to catch, swing, dodge, or let them pass.

My advice is to turn that chair around and take an appraising look in the mirror. Do you have what it takes to land your ideal man? What do you have to offer? If you have something of equal value, there is a possibility of getting what you want. There are tons of men with loving hearts, ripped abdomens, and fat wallets who would love to find you if it makes sense.

The old adage says, "Behind every great man is a greater woman."

But for me, standing behind these men as they divulge their precious secrets has made *me* a much greater woman. From the meek to the maverick, my clients have convinced me they are not all vile. They fascinate me, and I find myself attracted to their polarity. A woman will insist that a man is her archnemesis, and at the same time admit that he is the object of her one unquenchable desire. We will never understand the opposition. Their reasoning, ideas, notions, and methods will remain forever foreign to us.

One thing I do know, though, is that there are thousands of nerve endings just above the ear on a human scalp. When I run my finger along the top of the ear to be sure I didn't miss any little hairs, it sends a sensation that leaves a man utterly defenseless. This is when he will tell me *anything* I want to know … and everything I really don't.

"If you want a happy ending, that depends, of course, on where you stop your story."
-Orson Wells

Photos of Stacie by Doug Heslep

Stacie Harmon, a full time mother and part-time stylist, still stands behind the chair three days a week near the gulf shores of Florida. She is the founder of Ninth Wave Motivation, a women's focus club that helps others set and achieve personal goals. Stacie has co-written a children's animation series that she hopes will find its way to the television screen. The cartoon teaches and reinforces morals and values through surf-related story context. Stacie still enjoys writing and can usually be found "happy snapping" pictures and frolicking on the beach and in the surf with her daughter, Savannah.

Stacie would love to hear your comments … www.stacieharmon.com

Jennifer Christiansen, instructor of Psychology and English, writes for both children and adults. Currently in the final stages of her doctorate degree in Higher Education and Adult Learning, her research emphasis explores senior citizens and social media technology. Her free time is spent finding new challenges and traveling through America and Europe. She lives by the beaches of Fort Myers, Florida with her husband and two dogs.

Keep your eyes open for Jennifer's name on plenty of bookshelves in the future.

Doug MacGregor has been a cartoonist for years, getting his professional start drawing editorial cartoons for the Norwich Bulletin in eastern Connecticut in 1980, eight years later he moved to Florida and began drawing for The News-Press in Fort Myers until 2011. Doug teaches creative cartooning to the young and young at heart. He is also a freelance artist, designer, and self published author of five children's books. When Doug is not at his drawing board you'll find him singing or playing his harmonica with local blues bands. He writes and records his own songs and enjoys making iMovies. For more information, check out his website … www.dougcreates.com

14446946R00055

Made in the USA
Charleston, SC
11 September 2012